THE MANLINESS OF CHRIST

THE
MANLINESS
of CHRIST

How the Masculinity of Jesus
Eradicates Effeminate Christianity

DALE PARTRIDGE

Relearn Press

PRESCOTT, ARIZONA

Published in Prescott, Arizona by Relearn.org
Written by Dale Partridge
Third Edition
Cover Image: Painting: "Young Woman Praying in Church" (1854) by Jules Breton.
Printed in the U.S.A.

Scripture quotations taken from the (NASB®) New American Standard Bible®, Copyright © 1960, 1971, 1977, 1995, 2020 by The Lockman Foundation. Used by permission. All rights reserved. lockman.org.

Relearn Press is the publishing division of Relearn.org. For information, please contact us through our website at Relearn.org.

To my boys, Honor and Valor, if you want to see true manhood, don't look to me but to Christ. He is your mark. I am simply His slave whom He has blessed to raise you both.

Our Ministry

The mission of Relearn.org is simple:
To bring the church back to the Bible.
This is the driving force behind each of our
books, digital products, and podcasts.

Our Companion Ministries

MailTheGospel.org
ReformationSeminary.com
StandInVictory.org
UltimateMarriage.com
KingsWayBible.org

Table *of* Contents

FOREWORD

By Eric Conn

For well over a century, feminism has rotted through the once-stout timbers of Christianity in America. Starting in the early- to mid-1800s, the waves of feminism have rolled in, crashing upon churches whose pews have become predominantly occupied by women.

As a result, churches began attracting effeminate pastors—"inside boys" who couldn't cut it in a man's world—who catered their sermons to be more palatable to the feminine ear. There are a number of factors that caused this decline, which Ann Douglas catalogs in *The Feminization of American Culture.*

One contributing factor to the success of feminism in the church was the reduction of bold, Reformed preaching from men who demonstrated biblical patriarchy and faithful leadership in religious life. What replaced it was unitarianism, egalitarianism, and other liberal traditions built on emotionalism and storytelling rather than rich theology. This was a natural deterrent for strong men who were looking for doctrine and vision for building families and fighting against the culture.

In his book, Dale Partridge highlights the significant and often unnoticed impact of feminism on American Christianity. He emphasizes that many of us have unknowingly adopted a feminine perspective when reading the Bible, perceiving Christ primarily as meek, gentle, and mild. This has led to a prevalence of effeminate pastors and congregations predominantly composed of women, who embrace a feminized image of Jesus. Partridge argues that this selective portrayal of Christ neglects the portions of Scripture that depict His aggressive, courageous, and sacrificial manliness. Consequently, strong men have felt alienated from the church, creating a gap in male participation.

To be candid, there's often a discomfort that arises when we encounter Scripture passages that depict violence, aggression, or courageous acts from men. Take, for example, the account of Samson, who ingeniously bound 300 foxes together and set their tails on fire, causing havoc among the Philistines. Some may perceive this as an instance of toxic masculinity and conveniently attribute it to the Old Testament. However, let's not forget Jesus' actions in the New Testament when He braided a whip and drove people out of the temple or when He calls the Pharisees "sons of hell." His disciples remembered His actions as motivated by zealous righteousness, far from "gentle Jesus" who only has a passive demeanor. Such instances challenge the narratives of feminist theologians who seek to revise the biblical narrative.

Dale's insight is spot on: Jesus truly embodies the epitome of masculinity. He exemplifies *praus*, a Greek term often translated as meekness, which fails to convey the deeper meaning of "strength under control." Namely, Jesus was not weak. Rather, He is the perfect example of power and restraint. Therefore, it's time for us to shed the image of Jesus as a long-haired, feminine figure seeking humanitarian acts of kindness. Instead, we must reclaim a balanced, biblically grounded perspective that aligns with the teachings of Scripture.

This concise and impactful book has already resonated with thousands of men. It gets straight to the point, addressing the issue of feminism and impotence within our churches. It highlights how the imbalanced portrayal of Jesus in preaching and teaching has led to a lack of masculine congregations. It's time to confront the prevailing effeminacy in our churches, and this book offers a remedy.

May God raise up a generation of men who embrace *The Manliness of Christ* leading to a profound transformation in our homes, churches, and communities.

Eric Conn
CEO, New Christendom Press
Host, The Hard Men Podcast

CHAPTER

01

THE MARKS OF COURAGE

At just 18 years old, I witnessed a plane crash. I watched a six-seater Cessna fly vertically into a house splitting it in two. I quickly grabbed my father who was an airplane mechanic, we hopped into the car, and drove the short half-mile distance to the crash site.

Upon arrival, fuel was pouring down the driveway and the aircraft's engine was still running. My dad, knowing the risky circumstances of broken electrical, the engine's heat, and loose fuel looked at me and said, "I have to turn off that engine!" He ran into the rubble climbing some seven-to-ten feet into the divided two-story home and opened the cockpit. He immediately killed the engine and then checked the pulses of all the bloodied passengers—all four had died on impact. It was one of those moments in your life where you get to witness, in real-time, genuine masculinity.

Moments like this are everywhere in human history; each of them falling somewhere on a continuum of courage. While these acts can be carried out by both men and women, history confirms that resolve, courage, and bravery rest primarily in the masculine domain. The Apostle Paul even groups these traits together in the closing of the book of 1 Corinthians when he says, "Be watchful, stand firm in the faith, act like men, be strong. Let all that you do be done in love." (16:13-14). Combine this text with the hundreds of passages recording provision, battle, sacrifice, and honor and you quickly begin to see the intrinsic differences God has designed into the male genus. Yes, there is Deborah, Rahab, and Esther who demonstrated great courage, but they are far outnumbered by the courageous examples of men like Abraham, Joshua, Gideon, Sampson, David, the Mighty Men, Jonathan, Nehemiah, Daniel, the Prophets, the twelve Apostles, and Jesus Himself. Namely, the Bible is dripping with examples regarding male strength, boldness, courage, and responsibility. These moments range from short acts of valor to extraordinary displays of fortitude, but the harmonizing thread is rugged masculine virility.

In my research for this book, I noticed a link between many of these courageous acts. These links were often formed by a statement of necessity—a group of words that captures the commitment of the moment. For my dad, it was "I have to turn off that engine." For Martin Luther it was, "Here I stand. I can do no other. God help me. Amen."[1] For Winston Churchill it was, "We shall fight on the beaches, we shall fight on the landing grounds, we shall fight in the fields and in the streets, we shall fight in the hills, but we shall never surrender."[2] For the early church martyr Ignatius of Antioch, who was sentenced to death by lions, it was, "May I enjoy the wild beasts that are prepared for me. I pray that they would be found eager to rush at me, and I will also entice them to devour me speedily... If they are unwilling to assail me, I will compel them to do so."[3] History (both biblical and secular) is saturated with incredible stories of resolved men making valiant statements that precede powerful acts. These acts have become inspirational records illustrating commitment to God or values or morals in the face of pain, terror, and even death.

But of all the statements demonstrating the raw masculinity recorded in human history, there is none remotely more courageous than the words of Jesus in Matthew 20:18 where he says, "Behold, we are going up to Jerusalem." Just seven words. At face value, they are not unique or extreme. Grammatically, they form a simple phrase in the future tense. Descriptively, they are directional, unremarkable, and flat. But

---

1   Roland H. Bainton, *Here I Stand: A Life of Martin Luther* (Nashville: Abington Press, 2013).

2   Curtis Brown, "We Shall Fight on the Beaches," International Churchill Society, https://winstonchurchill.org/resources/speeches/1940-the-finest-hour/we-shall-fight-on-the-beaches/.

3   Paul A. Boer Sr., *St. Ignatius of Antioch* (Create Space Publishing, 2012).

behind these words, lies a degree of masculine resolve which no man can ever rival.

These words, without a doubt, make up the greatest and most dauntless statement made in the history of the world.

But unfortunately, the modern church has altogether missed it. Like the flyover territory of air travel, this pinnacle moment has been read over without any notoriety or consideration. But why? Why has the church not seen what I'm about to present? How have we missed what may be the most masculine act of Jesus' life?

My argument is this: Due to the effeminization of Jesus, the cultural hatred of masculinity, and the lack of faithful exposition in the pulpit we have been conditioned to not recognize the potent manliness and courageousness of Christ.

We, as a church, are certainly able to see such attributes in Daniel, Joshua, or Sampson. We firmly accept them in David's war chronicles and the decapitation of Goliath. But, for some reason, we are unwilling to see it in Christ's ministry and the decapitation of the serpent of sin (which I will discuss later).

In this short book, I will attempt to unearth and reveal the fierce, *manliness of Christ*. To accomplish this, I will first reveal how the culture and modern church has misrepresented

Jesus as a delicate deity. Second, I'll focus on his maleness and masculinity as both sacrificial Lamb and conquering Lion. Third, I will define the sin of effeminacy and how Jesus rejected it. Finally, I will bring to light what the church can learn from Jesus' masculinity and how the people of God can return to a biblical balance of masculine and feminine Christianity.

CHAPTER

02

THE DELICATE DEITY

THE DELICATE DEITY

Both the culture and the modern church have done an excellent job at misrepresenting the biblical Jesus.

As a culture, we have largely produced a caricature of Christ based on the anemic and soft-smiled Roman Catholic paintings where Jesus looks like He's just put on a fresh coat of blush and tweezed His eyebrows. Add the rise of feminism, the deconstructionist movement, and the progressive church and you end up with a delicate Jesus who's "knocking gently on the door of your heart." But it goes much further than this. Our modern culture despises masculinity. In fact, any form of masculinity that doesn't adhere to the world's standard is deemed "toxic."[1] There's a reason Ariana Grande's song "God is a Woman" was number one on Billboard's Top 100 list.[2]

---

1   Wikipedia, "Toxic Masculinity," 2020, https://en.m.wikipedia.org/wiki/Toxic_masculinity.

2   Gary Trust, "Ariana Grande Hits No. 1 On Pop Songs Chart With 'God Is a Woman,' Goes Top 10 With 'Breathin,' Billboard", https://www.billboard.com/pro/ariana-grande-god-is-a-woman-no-1-pop-songs-chart/.

The world is Hellbent on distorting, perverting, and redefining any biblical comprehension of gender whatsoever—to think this won't pervert our generation's view of the maleness of Jesus is just plain naive.

Unfortunately, the pulpit hasn't helped, either. For the past 30-50 years, the church has been infatuated with keynote Christianity where infotainers crack jokes and sprinkle in Scripture. As a result, these pulpiteers have left thousands of congregations with a Christ the people want but not the Christ that God sent. In truth, we have made a Jesus in our own image. Consequently, we are left with a Christology where Jesus is portrayed as some divine doormat who passively submits to the cross and begs people to "accept Him" as their Savior. In fact, I recently saw a viral social media graphic where fragile Jesus was in a hospital bed in heaven with a transfusion bloodline down to the world that read, "If they would only believe." What a falsification of Christ!

The truth is, Christ is not passive but active. He is not in distress, He is predominant. He is not subject, but King! Christ is not begging people to believe, He is sovereignly and mercifully saving those who are His and leaving the rest to eternal judgment (Eph. 1:4-5; Rom. 8:28-30, 9:11, 9:22; 1

Pet. 2:7-8). The modern church does not see this side of Jesus because most Christians define Christ by what they have heard and not by what they have read. We cannot know our Savior by only allowing other people to tell us who He is. We must, at some point, commit to opening our own Bibles and allowing the Scriptures alone to define Him.

Ultimately, we have a generation who has not only misrepresented Jesus in His sovereignty but has also robbed him of His masculinity. We have not seen Him as our all-powerful King, nor have we seen Him as a masculine Man. As a result, we have produced a version of Christianity that lives up to the Christ we have created—weak, effeminate, delicate, and soft. However, this is not the Christ of the Bible. As we will see in the following chapter, the biblical Jesus is not delicate or feminine; He is a 100% red-blooded male.

CHAPTER

03

THE MALENESS OF CHRIST

THE MALENESS OF CHRIST

Jesus was a man—conceived by a virgin, born biologically male, raised by a carpenter, a boy wise beyond his years (Luke 2:41-52), fully divine (John 1:1), and potently masculine. In fact, if you hate masculinity, you will despise the biblical Jesus.

He wasn't interested in "getting to know His feminine side" nor was He the macho and chauvinistic domineer that some failing men have become. Jesus was the epitome of manhood—a stalwart in mission, bold, obedient to the point of death, fearless in His proclamation of truth, sacrificial in His acts of love, and resolved to do His Father's will. Jesus had force, authority, and control in a way that marked Him as virile and robust.

Yes, it is true that our Lord also exemplified gentler traits, but these marks are not effeminate in nature they are, in proper placement, attributes of true masculinity. Historically, some theologians have claimed that Jesus is the perfect amalgam of man and woman. The 19th century English divine F.W. Robertson once said, "There is in Him the woman heart—as well as the manly brain."[3] Namely, he is claiming Jesus to be a pure breed image of God. This, of course, is true. But there is a nuance in Robertson's treatment which I believe, at a scholarly level, has injured the full maleness of Christ. I believe he has projected Adam's biological state upon Jesus. Namely, it's thought by many that Adam, prior to the extraction of Eve from his makeup, held within himself a more accurate representation of Robertson's definition.

That is, the newly created Adam was sexually male but intrinsically housed the source code of the masculine *and* feminine. As Dr. Alastair Roberts of Durham University put it, "The woman's being derives from the man's, the man's being from the earth—the *adamah*. Adam was 'formed' while Eve was 'built.'"[4]

This is both faithful exposition and wise logic. Prior to the "building" of Eve, Adam was the raw material for such a divine task. However, in a world in which woman already exists, this cannot be said equally of Christ's biology. He, unlike Adam, was born of a woman in the same way we are.

---

3 J.R. Miller, "The Manliness of Jesus" GraceGems.org, https://www.gracegems. org/Miller/manliness_of_jesus.htm. See also fwrobertson.org for a collection of his 19th century sermons.

4   Alastair Roberts, "Man and Woman in Creation (Genesis 1 and 2)", 9Marks, December 10, 2019, https://www.9marks.org/article/man-and-wom-an-in-creation-genesis-1-and-2/.

Furthermore, to claim that Christ has some unique form of masculine-feminine biology is to severely wound the Doctrine of the Hypostatic Union. Hebrews 2:14-18 [NASB] clearly states (bold for emphasis):

> "Since therefore the children share in flesh and blood, he himself likewise partook of the **same things**, that through death he might destroy the one who has the power of death, that is, the devil, and deliver all those who through fear of death were subject to lifelong slavery. For surely it is not angels that he helps, but he helps the offspring of Abraham. Therefore he had to be made like his brothers in **every respect** so that he might become a merciful and faithful high priest in the service of God, to make propitiation for the sins of the people. For because he himself has suffered when tempted, he is able to help those who are being tempted."

The crux of this passage is the result clause in verse 17 that states, "Therefore he had to be made like his brothers in *every respect*…" An alternative translation is "in all things." This does not mean Christ must be made like us in our spiritual state of sin and the effects thereof (wicked affections, sickness, disease, and death) but He must be made like us in our physical state (biologically human, and in His case, male).

For since the human species fell into sin under the Law only another human (not an angel or animal) born under the Law could redeem humanity through perfect obedience to the Law and sacrificial propitiation to satisfy the justice of the Law. This is the clear teaching of Paul in Galatians 4:4-5 when he said, "But when the fullness of time had come, God sent forth his Son, born of woman, born under the law, to redeem those who were under the law, so that we might receive adoption as sons."

I say all this to defend against the idea that Christ had some special or extraordinary emotional, hormonal, dual-gender physiology. We, as humans, certainly know that biological males do not have a "woman heart" and a "manly brain." No, males have a manly heart and a manly brain. Therefore, in His human nature, Christ exhibited the characteristics of a *typical* male.

For that reason, I argue that Jesus was fully and naturally a masculine man. In fact, He was the most masculine man who ever lived. But how was His masculinity expressed and what can the modern church learn from His example? The answer to these questions will be the focus of the following chapter.

CHAPTER

04

THE MASCULINITY OF CHRIST

THE MASCULINITY OF CHRIST

Men must primarily learn masculinity from Jesus. For this reason, I perform a short evening catechism with my boys.

I often include two questions: What do men do? My oldest sons (whose names are Honor and Valor) both respond "They protect and provide!" Next, I ask: Who is the only perfect man? "Jesus Christ!" they yell. Through further discussion, I attempt to demonstrate, in the simplest of ways, how Christ is the world's premier Provider and Protector. That is, I explain how He provides salvation at the expense of His own life and how He protects His Church from the attacks of the enemy and the grip of sin. But this is merely fingers deep into the ocean of Christ's masculinity. This concentrated exhibition of manhood manifests itself in five primary ways: His Boldness, His Fearlessness, His Intensity, His Sacrificial Love, and His Resolve. Let's briefly review each of them.

1. The Boldness of Jesus

The opposite of boldness is ambiguity. Many Christians today dance around hard issues using fuzzy language to communicate clear positions in Scripture. In short, we have an affection for improper prudery, political correctness, and apprehension. This was not true of Jesus. Standing before thousands of people He turns and says to them:

> "If anyone comes to me and does not hate his own father and mother and wife and children and brothers and sisters, yes, and even his own life, he cannot be my disciple. Whoever does not bear his own cross and come after me cannot be my disciple. So, therefore, any one of you who does not renounce all that he has cannot be my disciple." (Luke 14:26-27, 33)

Jonathan Edwards in his work *Religious Affections* once said, "Boldness enables Christians to forsake all rather than Christ, and to prefer to offend all rather than to offend Him."[5] That is, at the center of Christ's boldness is the commitment to please the Father no matter the cost. Namely, He was willing to speak God's truth in love regardless of the relational or physical consequences. Now the culture will surely cry, "Boldness is not a gender issue!' In one sense, this is correct. All people

---

5   Jonathan Edwards. *Religious Affections* (Moscow, ID: Canon Press, 2020).

can exhibit boldness. However, in the Bible, the character trait of boldness rests broadly upon the shoulders of men. In fact, the Scriptures even instruct the opposite character trait for a woman, "Let your adorning be the hidden person of the heart with the imperishable beauty of a gentle and quiet spirit, which in God's sight is very precious"(1 Pet. 3:4). That is, Christian women are to be in spiritual submission to their fathers, husbands, or elders. Biblical boldness, however, implies one to be out front by the will of God (as Christ was). The Oxford Dictionary lists one definition as "Willing to meet danger." This was characteristic of Jesus' ministry. He was a righteous provocateur! He was not afraid to challenge the status quo and confront evil. His boldness stemmed from His unwavering commitment to obeying the will of God. As Christian men, we are called to emulate His example, especially when it comes to proclaiming the Gospel and speaking out against the wickedness of our day.

In my research on boldness, I found that every New Testament command for a particular individual to be bold or have boldness (παρρησια or *parrésia*) was a descriptive or prescriptive act of a male. Namely, biblical boldness is clearly an attribute associated with men. So, when we think of boldness, let us not limit our perspective to historical figures like Churchill, Lincoln, Luther or Athanasius of Alexandria. Instead, let us first and foremost think of Jesus—the boldest Man who ever lived.

2. The Fearlessness of Christ

Fearlessness is the anchor of boldness. They cannot rightly operate without one another. That is to say, beneath the boldness of Christ is the sheer fearlessness of man. Sinclair Ferguson once said, "The fear of the Lord tends to take away all other fears. This is the secret of Christian courage."[6] I believe this to be true. But more importantly, I believe Jesus believed this to be true. Psalm 19:9 in the KJV says, "The fear of the Lord is clean…" Namely, the fear of the Lord is based in love and not in wrath. It is a reverential form of fear. Christ was not frightened by the Father but He righteously reverenced the Father. Hebrews 5:7 says, "In the days of His flesh, Jesus offered up prayers and supplications, with loud cries and tears, to Him who was able to save him from death, and He was heard because of His *reverence*." The fear of man, however, is a product of sin. 1 John 4:18 clues us in to how Jesus could live without this fear. The Apostle says, "There is no fear in love, but perfect love casts out fear." Because of Christ's divinity and His complete union with God and His love, He had unfettered fearlessness. He was known for unflinching and intense remarks and responses to godless men. Additionally, Christ fearlessly faced the devil himself, cast out demons, condemned religious leaders, and even

---

6   Sinclair Ferguson. *Grow in Grace* (Carlisle, PA: Banner of Truth, 1989), 33- 34.

faced the horrors of the cross. But more than that, He was able to authoritatively command others to "fear not." That is, He could command such fearlessness because there was not one molecule of hypocrisy in Him. Christ was not timid. He was completely fearless—a foundational trait of masculinity.

Proverbs 29:25 declares, "The fear of man lays a snare, but whoever trusts in the Lord is safe." In this verse, Solomon imparts wisdom about the detrimental consequences of placing undue importance on human opinions, a quality that was never seen in the ministry of Christ. While this teaching applies to all individuals, it carries particular significance for men. As men, we are called to embody the words of Paul in Romans 8:31, "If God is for us, who can be against us?" and the words of John in his first epistle, "Greater is He who is in you than he who is in the world."

Jesus exemplified fearlessness through His perfect communion with God. Through the Gospel, this fearlessness becomes a reality for us as well. Through the perfect redemption we have received in Christ, we are liberated from fear. This attribute is essential for faithful leadership in a fallen world, and it is a trait that must be nurtured in the church by God's grace. We need more men who are unafraid because they fear the Lord above all else.

3. The Intensity of Christ

I recently posted a video on social media of a Christian man walking into a drag queen story hour where little children were being indoctrinated with debauchery. The man was intense. He walked into the room passionately condemning the wickedness before him while, at the same time, preaching a clear Gospel of repentance and belief in Christ alone. While he was loud, firm, and unrelenting, he did not use foul language, threats, or inflict physical harm upon anyone.

Within a few hours, I had several comments from people saying, "This is not the way to win people to Jesus," and "This does not represent Christ," and "He should have approached this with a softer spirit." Essentially, people implied this man's anger against sin and passion for righteousness were not representative of Christ. Namely, they wonder how this man's intensity can be akin to the meek, tender, and merciful Jesus we see in the Scriptures?

For many decades, emotionalism has crept into the church, taking weak-minded Christians captive. They believe that the love of Christ is not seen in the hatred of evil. However, they are unaware of Proverbs 8:13, which specifically says, "The fear of the Lord is *hatred of evil*." My friend Kangmin Lee recently took notice of this reality when he wrote, "Americanized Christianity has convinced millions of professing Christians that 'love your enemies' means 'have no enemies.' This has resulted in the church becoming apathetic toward, and tolerant of, unbridled evil."

Again, our model is not some modernized caricature of Christ, but the biblical Christ. So the question becomes, how did Jesus respond to those who upheld evil, taught false doctrine, deceived children, willfully stood against the Kingdom of God, and perverted or distorted the worship of His Father? Did He quietly respond with, "Excuse me, what you're doing is incorrect," or "Are you aware that you are sinning?" No. Instead, He invokes intense, aggressive, and cutting language to publicly shame, convict, and even condemn those who stand against God. He calls them (to their face) hypocrites and liars (Matt. 23:13, John 8:55). He calls them a brood of vipers (Matt. 23:33). He calls them children of Satan (John 8:44), sons of hell (Matt. 23:15), a wicked and adulterous generation (Matt 16:4), whitewashed tombs (Matt. 23:27-28), fools (Luke 24:25; Matt. 23:17), and blind guides (Matt. 15:14). Ultimately, there is another side of the compassionate Jesus—an intense, angry, mocking, and even satirical side of our Savior.

But Jesus' hatred of evil goes further than strong words. In John 2:13-17, we see Jesus filled with righteous anger toward the perversion of worship. During Passover, the temple courts were filled with the salesman of livestock for the thousands of anticipated sacrifices. Where is Jesus? Braiding a whip in preparation to drive out herds of animals and disrupt this moment of blasphemy. But He doesn't stop there. He begins flipping over the tables of the merchants who attempted to profit off of worship. He grabbed their money and threw it on the ground. In other words, Jesus, while kind and gentle to *His sheep*, was fierce toward those who perpetuated evil, false religion, and deception. John Calvin understood this when he wrote, "The pastor ought to have two voices: one, for gathering the sheep; and another, for warding off and driving away wolves and thieves. The Scripture supplies him with the means of doing both."[7]

So looking back to the example of the man who had zealously disrupted the drag queen story hour, we see his statements of moral condemnation and proclamations of the Gospel are directly in-step with the character of Christ. That is, he was more like Christ in that moment than much of today's painfully silent Christian men. Now, Jesus was a perfect man. Namely, in these moments of intensity, He exemplified the ability to run to the edge of anger without sinning. He also demonstrated how to walk the line of compassion without enabling transgression. But what men must learn from Him is that, in a world where evil has been permitted to flourish by the silence of the church, we must stand aggressively, boldly, truthfully, and lovingly against evil. We must be willing to open our mouths against those who

---

7 Calvin, John. 2014. Institutes of the Christian Religion. Translated by Robert White. Edinburgh, Scotland: Banner of Truth Trust.

sustain and preserve cultural evils like false religion, abortion, homosexuality, transgenderism, feminism, and pornography. Evil must know that there is a wall of righteousness, and it will not be penetrated. Jesus said, "The gates of hell will not prevail against the Church" (Matt. 16:17). Therefore, let us live as men who walk in this prophesied victory. Through Christ, we can confidently condemn evil and stand for truth. Through Christ, we can confidently call out wickedness and preach the Gospel. Through Christ, we can have anger without sin and compassion without tolerance. Ultimately, as Christian men, we can be intense—as long as it's through the power of Christ and Christ alone.

4. The Sacrificial Love of Christ

In today's culture, love has more counterfeits than money. Our society is brimming with pithy catchphrases like "Love is love" or "Love wins" or "Love yourself" that attempt to put forth a definition that is all-accepting, all-tolerant, and all-liberating. But the river of love must flow down the banks of truth. The truth is, love has a definition. 1 Corinthians 13:4-8 states, "Love is patient and kind; love does not envy or boast; it is not arrogant or rude. It does not insist on its own way; it is not irritable or resentful; it does not rejoice at wrongdoing, but rejoices with the truth. Love bears all things, believes all things, hopes all things, endures all things. Love never ends."

In short, love is not based on superficial feelings but on sacrificial commitment. We cannot accept culture's fraudulent substitutes. Jesus in John 10:11 says, "I am the good shepherd. The good shepherd lays down his life for the sheep." At the core of love, we see sacrifice. But at the core of sacrifice, we see true masculinity. In Ephesians 5:25 Paul instructs: "Husbands, love your wives, as Christ loved the church and gave himself up for her…" To be clear, this is not a two-way street. There is no passage of Scripture telling women to sacrifice themselves for men. Sure, there is a general principle of sacrificial love which can be applied by all; but men, like Christ, are called to sacrifice themselves for their women—specifically their wives. However, this does not mean men sacrifice their duty to lead to permit their wives to take charge. For example, I recently had a young man tell me that he sacrificed his dream of starting a business so his wife could go to Seminary and start a ministry. While this act may appear sacrificial, it does not align with the biblical concept of sacrificial love and servant leadership. Biblical servant leadership is *service by leadership*.[8] It's a man who sacrifices his carnal pleasures so that he can fulfill his God-given duty to lead, provide, and protect the women in his life.

---

8 Tennant, Bnonn. 2019. "Servant Leadership Transforms Leadership into Subservience — It's Good to Be a Man." It's Good to Be a Man. May 9, 2019. https://itsgoodtobeaman.com/servant-leadership-transforms-leadership-into-subservience/.

But you may be wondering, "How is sacrificial love masculine?" To put it briefly, love forms the basis for any proper fight. The masculine desire to protect is fueled by the love of one's own. Namely, we battle for what is ours to guard. Shepherds are to guard the flock that has been entrusted to them (Acts 20:28). Men are to protect and provide for their families (1 Tim. 5:8). G.K. Chesterton once wrote, "The true soldier fights not because he hates what is in front of him, but because he loves what is behind him."[9]

This is Christ to the core. Jesus came to fight and sacrifice Himself—not for all but for those who are His. He didn't sacrifice Himself for everyone, but for His bride—the Church (Eph. 5:25-27). He didn't sacrifice Himself for each and every person, but for the sheep (John 10:11, 15).

Matthew 1:21 says of Mary, "She will bear a son, and you shall call his name Jesus, for he will save *his people* from their sins." Jesus came to sacrifice Himself for His people. The cross was His aim. He was spiritually and biologically designed for it. It was masculine, sacrificial love on grand display. There is no greater example and men must learn to follow it.

5. The Resolve of Christ

If sacrificial love was the rose of Christ then His resolve is its

---

9 G.K. Chesterton, "War and Politics," The Society of G.K. Chesterton, Originally said in the Illustrated London News, Jan. 14, 1911, https://www. chesterton.org/quotations/war-and-politics/.

stem. That is to say, the beauty of the cross is elevated when we see what drove it.

Theologically speaking, it was our sin that induced the cross. It was God's love that compelled the cross. But it was Christ's resolve that made the cross so beautiful.

Resolve, by definition, refers to firmly deciding on a course of action. When we consider the cross, it becomes evident that it was not a mere event in time; rather, it was a deliberate and divine choice. Namely, the divine Trinity was not obligated to select this course of redemptive action. There were no grounds to justify such a choice. Yet, in His sovereign wisdom, God chose this path, and Jesus was born for the purpose of fulfilling it. In a very real sense, His mission was not life, but death!

John Stott in his renowned work *The Cross of Christ* said, "What dominated his mind was not the living but the giving of His life."[10] Christ *chose* the cross! In the truest sense, He ran to it. This is not seen more clearly than in Mark 10:32-34 which states:

"And they were on the road, going up to Jerusalem, and

---

10   John Stott. *The Cross of Christ* (Downers Grove, IL: Intervarsity Press, 2006), 37.

Jesus was walking ahead of them. And they were amazed, and those who followed were afraid. And taking the twelve again, he began to tell them what was to happen to him, saying, 'See, we are going up to Jerusalem, and the Son of Man will be delivered over to the chief priests and the scribes, and they will condemn him to death and deliver him over to the Gentiles. And they will mock him and spit on him, and flog him and kill him."

Do not miss the words "and Jesus was walking ahead of them." This was a remarkable display of resolute masculinity. The moment was drenched with courage. Webster defines courage as "not deterred by danger or pain." This was certainly an expression of just that. Christ knew exactly what was going to happen to Him. He knew of the spitting, beating, whipping, and nailing that was about to come. But more than that, He knew of the wrath of God He would endure for the sins of His people. He knew of the coming anguish and horror of being forsaken by the Father. He knew of the unspeakable and, for us, unknowable agony of divine penalty. And where was Jesus? Walking ahead of them! He would not be deterred or deflected. He would not be intimidated. He was resolved to accomplish His mission—to save His people from their sins.

Now, like all the attributes we've discussed, resolve is not limited to the masculine realm. However, the highlights of heroic history exude moments of male resolve. When it comes to persevering through difficult, risky, traumatic, and bloody tasks, men take the crown. Elizabeth Hoisington, one of the first women to attain the rank of Brigadier General in the U.S. Army says:

"I do not doubt the Army has women who can complete a combat course, endure three days or three weeks under field conditions, and shoot as straight as any man. But in my whole lifetime, I have never known 10 women whom I thought could endure three months under actual combat conditions in an Army unit. Women cannot match men in aggressiveness, physical stamina, resolve, and muscular strength in long-term situations."[11]

This is not shocking information. An intellectual person cannot deny the science that demonstrates the biological advantage that testosterone offers in moments of resolve in the face of death. A team of researchers from a 2018 study in Wales concluded, "The striking male post-pubertal increase in circulating testosterone (15-30 times higher than women) provides a major, ongoing, cumulative, and durable phys-

---

11   Debra Bell, "Debate: Should Women Fight in War," U.S. News & World Report, February 13, 1978. Digital Version: https://www.usnews.com/news/blogs/press-past/2013/05/15/arguing-for-and-against-women-incombat-in-1978.

ical advantage in sporting contests by creating larger and stronger bones, greater muscle mass and strength, and higher circulating hemoglobin as well as possible psychological differences."[12]

Therefore, it is important to recognize that Christ's resolute determination throughout His passion ministry was greatly enabled by His physical form. At a physiological level, God chose to send His Son Jesus into the world in the form of a man, equipped with a male body capable of enduring the physical hardships, displaying boldness and steadfastness through his supply of testosterone, and having an emotional and mental state that could withstand the curses, insults, and deceptions. God purposefully endowed Him with the masculine qualities required to fulfill His earthly responsibilities as the Messiah. The modern world would likely deem the rough side of Jesus' masculinity "toxic" and the soft side of His masculinity "effeminate"; however, He was neither. Instead, Christ exemplified a perfect display of masculinity that is worthy of every man's admiration.

---

12   David J Handelsman, Angelica L Hirschberg, and Stephane, "Circulating Testosterone as the Hormonal Basis of Sex Differences in Athletic Performance" NCBI, July 13, 2018, https://www.ncbi.nlm.nih.gov/pmc/articles/PMC6391653/#__ffn_sectitle.

CHAPTER

05

THE SIN OF EFFEMINACY

THE SIN OF EFFEMINACY

On the cover of the March 2018 edition of *The Hollywood Reporter*, you will find four men dressed in prim clothing standing in line with their right hand in the pocket of the man in front of them. The headline reads, "Triumph of the Beta Male." It's very effeminate.

Today's culture has celebrated effeminacy among men. More and more guys are adopting the "gay look" and employing not only a womanish exterior but also embracing foppish interiors and emotional constitutions. This movement is a disease attacking the tenants of masculinity and distorting God's intention for manhood.

Many think effeminacy is an issue of a person's nature. That it's an untaught disposition, and we should not seek to reform its characteristics. This, of course, is built upon the idea that effeminacy is a morally neutral characteristic among men. But it's not.

In Paul's letter to the Corinthians, the Apostle is dealing

with a profoundly immoral and disordered church in Corinth. It's been described as a letter of Christian ethics because it deals so heavily with practical matters for a debauched society. This generation can learn much from this great book.

In 1 Corinthians 6, Paul is demonstrating the sinfulness of Christians taking other Christians to court—especially before a pagan judge. He was attempting to show how unrighteous it was for a person to detach their Christianity from their civil life. In verses 9-10, he reminds them that unrighteous acts are not characteristic of those who profess Christ. He provides a list of those evil individuals and declares their station to be outside of the Kingdom of God. However, in his list, he includes one class of individuals we often overlook—"the effeminate." The text reads:

> "Or do you not know that the unrighteous will not inherit the kingdom of God? Do not be deceived; neither fornicators, nor idolaters, nor adulterers, **nor effeminate**, nor homosexuals, nor thieves, nor the covetous, nor drunkards, nor revilers, nor swindlers, will inherit the kingdom of God." - 1 Corinthians 6:9-10

For years, I missed this term because the English Standard Version, as well as the NKJV and NIV, translates the word into either one clause, "nor men who practice homosexuality," or into two synonymous terms, "nor homosexuals, nor sodomites." But the NASB95 and the Legacy Standard Bible (LSB) get it right. In Greek, it says, "οὔτε μαλακοὶ, οὔτε ἀρσενοκοῖται" which literally means "nor effeminate, nor homosexuals."

Unmasking Effeminacy

The word "μαλακοὶ" or *malakoi* is translated into our English word "effeminate." It's also a *hapax legomena* which means it's a word that only appears once in the entire Bible.

The word is an adjective derived from the Greek word *malakos*, which means "soft" or "loose." In Greek, it doesn't have a phonetic relationship with "femininity" as it does in English. In the context of 1 Corinthians 6:9, "*malakoi*" refers to men who were morally weak and had a failing will (which, as we know, is more common in women; 1 Tim. 2:14; 2 Cor. 11:3; cf. Gen 3:1-6). It is speaking to a malfunction in men causing them withdraw from the pursuit of good and, instead, seek pleasure. In a sense, to be effeminate is to adopt traits uncharacteristic of masculinity, which makes an important distinction for our discussion. A woman cannot be effeminate; only a man can. A woman acting like a woman is "feminine" (and right). But a man acting like a woman is "effeminate" and wrong.

In the first century, this term would have been understood

as those men who avoided work and battle and preferred comfort or luxury. They are those who were delicate and inappropriately tender. They were not those men who, like Christ, were intense, bold, courageous, controlled, resolved, meek, and enduring in the face of adversity or pain.

The lesson of the text is that morally soft men are unrighteous. They are out of step with God's design for the masculine domain. They are adopters of compromise, they are unsteady, and they are controlled by their emotions.

Luxury, Softness, and Their Tangled Bond

Luxury and softness share a profound connection. In the biblical world, luxury was defined as the excessive indulgence of specific desires and the unproductive utilization of valuable resources. For instance, individuals who would hoard precious possessions or exquisite items without utilizing their value for the betterment of others were a mark of effeminacy. This type of luxury, likely stemming from past softness, was also seen as the cause of softness itself. As men indulged in luxurious lifestyles, they often lost their moral compass in search of pleasure. Therefore, the association between luxury and effeminacy was apparent, as luxury-seeking increased, so did personal delicacy. [13]

---

13 Wedgeworth, Steven. 2018. Calvinist International. What is Effeminacy? July 2018. https://calvinistinternational.com/2018/07/15/what-is-effeminacy/.

Aristotle, who lived three centuries before Christ, speaks to the connection between softness and luxury. In his book on ethics, he says:

"The deliberate avoidance of pain is rather a kind of softness; the deliberate pursuit of pleasure is extravagance in the strict sense. Self-restraint is the opposite of unrestraint, and endurance is the opposite of softness; for endurance means only successful resistance, whereas restraint implies mastery, which is a different matter. Victory is more glorious than the mere avoidance of defeat. Hence self-restraint is a more valuable quality than endurance. One who is deficient in resistance to pains that most men withstand with success is soft or luxurious (for luxury is a kind of softness): such a man lets his cloak trail on the ground to escape the fatigue and trouble of lifting it, or pretends sickness, not seeing that to counterfeit misery is to be miserable."[14]

Softness or pleasure-seeking was seen as lacking the fortitude of masculinity. True men face pain as a way to build endurance. They do not avoid challenges or relinquish their responsibilities, regardless of the difficulties they may face.

The fourth-century church father, John Chrysostom, also

14 Aristotle. Nicomachean Ethics. Translated by H. Rackham. Loeb Classical Library 73. Cambridge, MA: Harvard University Press, 1926.

speaks to this dimension of effeminacy. In his 24th Homily, he comments on Romans 13:14, which says, "But put on the Lord Jesus Christ, and make no provision for the flesh, to gratify its desires." He says:

> "To gain a better understanding of what it means to make provision for fulfilling the lusts of the flesh and to avoid such provision, consider those who are given to excessive drinking, indulgent in food, obsessed with fashionable attire, effeminate in behavior, or leading a life of softness and relaxation. Their actions are not aimed at health, but rather at satisfying their base desires and arousing lust. As someone who has clothed themselves with Christ, it is crucial for you to remove such indulgences."[15]

It's clear that luxury, extravagance, and seeking accessory were characteristics of effeminate men. Engaging in self-ornamentation to attract external admiration or proudly displaying a life of leisure was not considered a mark of true manliness. This practice, both historically and in contemporary times, involves incorporating feminine traits into masculinity. It hinders men from fully carrying out their duties and responsibilities and undermines the true essence and definition of

---

15 Chrysostom, John. n.d. "Homily 24 on Romans." Newadvent.org. Accessed May 19, 2023. https://www.newadvent.org/fathers/210224.htm.

biblical manhood.

Jesus and the Effeminate

This negative outlook toward the soft and luxurious man was not merely a position held by Paul but also by Christ. In Luke 7:24-26, Jesus uses rhetorical questions to demonstrate the contrast between the idealized view of a prophet and the raw reality of a man like John the Baptist. The text says:

> "Jesus began to speak to the crowds concerning John: 'What did you go out into the wilderness to see? A reed shaken by the wind? What then did you go out to see? A man dressed in soft clothing? Behold, those who are dressed in splendid clothing and live in luxury are in kings' courts. What then did you go out to see? A prophet? Yes, I tell you, and more than a prophet."

Jesus criticizes those men who wore soft clothing and lived in luxury. He did so to cast down the view that effeminacy was associated with strength and power. Instead, He highlights that God's man—John the Baptist—was neither soft nor a seeker of comfort. John's lifestyle was far from luxury; he lived as a rugged and unconventional figure, living on locusts and wild honey, dressed in garments made of camel's hair with a leather belt around his waist (Mark 1:6). Jesus even proclaimed John as the "greatest man to be born of women" (Matthew 11:11). Thus, John's distinctive way of life stands in clear opposition to the effeminate character that the crowds expected to find.

Jesus was not much different than John. As the King of kings and Lord of lords, Christ's condescension to earth, born in a manger and raised by a carpenter, should always remind us of His humble masculine nature (Heb. 2:5-8; Luke 2:11-12; Matt. 13:55). He did not come to be served but to serve (Matt. 20:28). He did not come to rest but to work (John 5:17). He did not come to be adorned as King but to suffer for His people (Isaiah. 53). Jesus was certainly many things, but he was not soft or luxurious.

In Matthew 8:20, Jesus speaks to the cost of following Him. He says to a scribe, "Foxes have holes, and birds of the air have nests, but the Son of Man has nowhere to lay his head." Jesus was, in a very real sense, without the common comforts of ordinary life. I'm not saying this is the prescribed path for all men. I'm simply highlighting that Jesus was not one seeking ease or convenience. His life was marked with toughness and inconvenience. He was a man of productivity, efficiency, simple joys, relationships, and sacrificial servitude.

This should serve as a valuable lesson for Christian men who might have been enticed by the allure of worldly pleasures. In a culture that equates male success with indulgence, opulence, and ease, we can clearly discern that such pursuits do not align with the life of the ultimate Man, Jesus Christ.

While possessing nice things is not inherently sinful, a life consumed by the pursuit of material possessions is. In the eyes of men in ancient times, amassing a collection of cars, guns, or suits would have been deemed both extravagant and effeminate. Therefore, examine your life. Where have comfort and pleasure taken precedence over productivity and fruitfulness? Evaluate if you have adopted the posture of softness or luxury. Ask yourself how you can reorient your life toward action, faithfulness, and functionality.

Effeminacy as Sexual Deviancy

The final aspect of *malakoi* pertains to its association with sexual perversion. It is crucial to recognize that the pursuit of softness and luxury was not the origin of effeminacy but rather the result of it. The assumption of the text is that the underlying cause of effeminate behavior is perverted sexual desires. John Calvin speaks to this in his commentary on this passage. He says:

> "By effeminate persons, I understand those who, although they do not openly abandon themselves to impurity, discover, nevertheless, their unchastity by blandishments of speech, by lightness of gesture and apparel, and other

allurements."[16]

Effeminacy can be understood as the external expression of an internal distortion. While it is distinct from homosexuality, it encompasses the outward indicators commonly associated with it. To not mince words, Calvin is speaking about the "gay look," the lisp, and the feminine sway so common among sodomites. This is why it is crucial for us to firmly oppose the movement within the church that suggests that same-sex attraction is not sinful if a person remains celibate. In reality, same-sex attraction, as well as the gay mannerisms and effeminate characteristics in men, are distortions of the natural attractions, mannerisms, and characteristics of biblical masculinity. To permit a man who professes Christ to maintain his effeminate tendencies without being in sin is wrong. When God restores a person, He restores not only their heart and soul but also their mind. Namely, grace restores nature, and God's nature for men is unadulterated masculinity.

Ultimately, effeminacy involves adopting behaviors that are biblically associated with women, who are naturally characterized by their softness. The most extreme form of effeminacy is manifested in homosexuality, wherein a man willingly embraces the sexual role of a woman. By choosing to abandon the pursuit of true masculinity, he deviates from

---

16 Calvin, John. 2022. Commentary, Vol. 1: On the Epistles of Paul the Apostle to the Corinthians (Classic Reprint). London, England: Forgotten Books.

his intended design as a man. Such actions, whether by mere mannerism or by sodomy, are sinful and are not indicative of those who have experienced true regeneration.

Conclusion

At the close of Paul's first letter to the Corinthians, he writes, "Be on the alert, stand firm in the faith, act like men, be strong." This demonstrates Paul's concern for male orthodoxy. He condemns effeminacy and calls for masculinity in the same letter. Steven Wedgeworth, in an article titled *What is Effeminacy?* writes on this verse:

> "An intriguing term is employed here to describe bravery, with a literal meaning of 'to show oneself to be a man": (*andrizesthe*). Notably, this verse also emphasizes the importance of perseverance: "Stand firm in the faith, show manliness, be strong."'[17]

In essence, Paul calls for the Corinthians to embrace the creational qualities of masculinity. He's saying, "Men, be what God made you to be. Act in accordance with your design. Be vigilant, reject softness, represent Christ, and demonstrate your strength to an onlooking world." Paul knows that effeminate Christians produce a dangerous example of manhood.

17 Wedgeworth, Steven. 2018. Calvinist International. What is Effeminacy? July 2018. https://calvinistinternational.com/2018/07/15/what-is-effeminacy/.

He knows that effeminacy is a disfigurement of the image and glory of God (1 Cor. 11:7). He knows that a man's posture tells people something about their Maker.

Ultimately, he knows the behavior of being effeminate contradicts the example set by Jesus. Thus, it becomes our responsibility to earnestly strive to reflect the true essence of Christ in our thoughts, actions, and choices. By doing so, we avoid misrepresenting Christ to an onlooking world. But most of all, we help reorient other men to male holiness and authentic masculinity.

CHAPTER

06

The Effeminate Church

THE EFFEMINATE CHURCH

David Murrow, the author of *Why Men Don't Go to Church* opens with a bold fact, "Christianity is the only world religion with a chronic shortage of men."

Brenda E. Brasher the author of *Godly Women* affirms this reality when she writes, "If American religion were imaginatively conceptualized as a clothing store, two-thirds of its floor space would house garments for women."[18]

Unfortunately, both of these statements are correct. Study after study affirms that women significantly outpace men in church attendance.[19] But why? One would think that having such a masculine Messiah would prevent such an effeminate

---

David Murrow. *Why Men Hate Going to Church* (Nashville: Thomas Nelson, 2011).

18   Brenda E. Brasher, *Godly Women: Fundamentalism and Female Power* (Chicago, IL: Rutgers University Press, 1997).

19   Dalia Fahmy. "Christian women in the U.S. are more religious than their male counterparts", Pew Research, April 6, 2018, https://www.pewresearch.org/fact-tank/2018/04/06/christian-women-in-the-u-s-are-more-religious-than-their-male-counterparts/.

local church. However, these results are not without basis. For the past 40-50 years, the church has drastically shifted from the historic expression of Christianity to an effeminate alternative. We have traded the fire and brimstone preaching of the early 20th century for the soft and encouraging Ted-Talk style infotainers of today. We have removed the pulpit that acted as a combat podium for God's preachers and replaced it with a high-top table with a flower arrangement. We have moved from classic hymns about doctrine and sacrifice and holiness to emotional love songs where people sway their hips to "Jesus Lover of My Soul."

As for the pastoral dress, the suit has gone to the garbage and has been replaced with skinny jeans, a necklace, and a swoop-cut shirt that looks like a repurposed woman's blouse. But it doesn't stop there, we have pastors using phrases like "Do life together" and "Love on each other" and "Let go and let God" and "Share what's on your heart." In addition, more churches are ordaining women as pastors which is a direct attempt to flip the biblical order of feminine submission to husbands, fathers, and biblical elders upside down. In short, we have, in a very real way, emasculated the local church.

The gender-role distortion and infatuation with egalitarianism have contributed to great confusion in the church of what it means to be a biblical man or woman. It has left women fighting for leadership and left men without direction in their role in marriage, church, and family. But more than that, it has left children without visible models of biblical masculinity and femininity. In fact, I strongly believe this has been the enemy's central strategy for this generation.

He has influenced the church to such a place of feminine emotion that when the time comes for masculine boldness, fearlessness, sacrifice, and resolve, the church (and culture) will be grossly unprepared.

Coffee shop and bookstore Christianity is no match for prison cell and angry mob Christianity.

The truth is, church history is saturated with Christians being tortured, dismembered, eaten, shot, hung, racked, boxed, buried, and burned for Christ. The timidity of the current church, which submits to government overreach and complies with laws enforcing unbiblical support of sexual sin, will be costly.

The time is coming soon when the need for masculine Christian men will be intense and their availability will be short. This should not shock anyone, either. The feminism movement of the 21st century is not about biblical female valuation, it's about male domination. Furthermore, by now we must see that their movement does not have borders. Like the LGBTQ community, they seek to saturate every facet of public, personal, and spiritual life. This should, at the very least, cause alarm to the current local church and, at the very most, prepare us to fight aggressively against it. Ultimately, we need both biblical shepherds and faithful women to see through the societal smoke and guard against this dangerous infiltration of effeminate culture.

Biblical Patriarchy

Lastly, we cannot forget that Christianity is not an egalitarian religion. Yes, men and women are equal in value before the cross, but we are not equal in our being or our duties. While we complement one another sexually, Christianity is patriarchal in marriage, family, church, and society.

Biblical womanhood expert Lori Alexander demonstrates this distinction when she wrote, "The church doesn't complete nor complement Christ. The church is under Christ's authority and obeys His commands, as a wife is under her husband's authority and obeys his commands. This is patriarchy as God intended it to be (Eph. 5:24; 1 Pet. 3:6; 1 Cor. 11:9,9)."

If anyone could have revised religious thinking on this issue and made women the model for leadership it was Jesus—yet He still chose twelve men. He did so because He knows men are not just called to lead but are anatomically, biologically, and hormonally *designed* to lead. He also knows that women should not lead because they *cannot* lead. Namely, women are not anatomically, biologically, and hormonally, designed for leadership but for helping and submitting. That is, it is not merely roles that distinguish our differences but our very being.

This generation, of course, abhors these truths surrounding biblical patriarchy. I admit that "patriarchy," like marriage, fatherhood, or heterosexuality, has the ability to express itself in unbiblical and sinful ways. However, these structures are good and fruitful when carried out in sacrificial love, biblical order, and for God's glory.

All that being said, we need both masculinity and femininity in their proper order. We must strive to align the gender culture of the church with the gender culture of Scripture. Namely, it should be strong, bold, biblical, and resolute, while at the same time compassionate, loving, and encouraging. When this balance is achieved, we witness the full manifestation of Christ in the church, and His people can march forward in step with their conquering Lord.

CHAPTER

07

The Masculine Church

THE MASCULINE CHURCH

This generation has selected their preferred qualities for Jesus—the gentle and lowly lamb, the suffering servant, and the loving Shepherd.

In fact, Dane Ortlund wrote a book titled "Gentle and Lowly," where he expounds upon this aspect of Christ. How did the book perform? The church gorged on it. At the time of this writing, it has nearly 11,000 reviews on Amazon (that's pretty incredible), it's a top 500 book on Amazon (which is even more incredible), and the publisher has put together several additional resources to fulfill the insatiable appetite for this perspective of Jesus. Now, to be clear, there is nothing heretical with this book. In fact, it's actually a faithful presentation of this dimension of Christ.

The problem is that every man is multi-dimensional, and Jesus is no exception. The truth is, the church has a disproportionate and incomplete view of Christ. Yes, Christ is gentle and lowly at heart, but He is also Victor over His enemies. Yes, Christ is the Suffering Servant, but He is also the Conquering King. Yes, Christ is a loving Shepherd, but He is also the God-Man who rules with authority, dominion, and power.

In essence, our church has prioritized the aspects of Christ that align with softness rather than strength, favoring traits such as gentleness, servanthood, and tenderness. While these qualities are indeed important and are part of a biblical masculine identity, they represent only a fraction of the broader spectrum of masculine characteristics.

But what the current church has clearly shut its eyes to is Christ's identity as Victor, Conqueror, and King. These are not primarily masculine traits; they are completely masculine traits. They are alpha positions of battle, command, and supremacy. Ultimately, the contemporary church has allowed the attributes of Jesus (gentle, tender, and loving) to overpower the identity of Jesus (Victor, Conqueror, and King).

This lopsided perspective of Christ is not benign, either. In fact, it has manifested itself in ways that have greatly influenced God's people and their witness to the world. The "gentle-and-lowly-only" Jesus—the Jesus this generation so obsessively promotes and preaches, has contributed greatly to the passive, non-combative, and submissive church culture of our day. The "loving-shepherd-only" Jesus has nurtured a culture of sin tolerance leading to the acceptance of behavior that Scripture condemns. Ultimately, I believe this unbalanced emphasis on Jesus has, in large part, rendered the non-threatening, pushover Christianity that's so prevalent in the West. experienced defeat in numerous moral battles over the past century, including issues concerning life, marriage, sexuality, and gender. The Christianity that opts predominantly for silence and softness instead of moral confrontation and action.

For those who study history, you know that in ancient times it was common for kings to lead their armies into battle. The posture of the king would greatly influence the culture of the troops. If their king was apprehensive, timid, or fearful of the enemy, the morale of the troops would follow in step. But if their king was aggressive, confident, and wise, the troops would be invigorated to triumph.

This truth is clearly seen in the difference between the kingship of Saul and David. In the famous account of Goliath's challenge to Israel, the giant stood up and shouted:

"Why have you come out to draw up for battle? Am I not a Philistine, and are you not servants of Saul? Choose a man for yourselves, and let him come down to me. If he is able to fight with me and kill me, then we will be your servants. But if I prevail against him and kill him, then you shall be our servants and serve us." And the Philistine said, "I defy the ranks of Israel this day. Give me a man, that we may fight together." When Saul and all Israel heard these words of the Philistine, they were dismayed and greatly afraid." (1 Sam. 17:8-11).

Case and point: The troops of Saul adopted the posture of their king—fear and defeat.

Then, young David walks onto the scene. He finds the entire encampment of Israel saturated with terror. In the distance he hears the source of their fright—the wicked and sinful claims of Goliath. His response was, "For who is this uncircumcised Philistine, that he should defy the armies of the living God?" (1 Sam. 17:26). Then, we see the correspondence between Saul and David that defines these two men:

"And David said to Saul, "Let no man's heart fail because of him. Your servant will go and fight with this Philistine." And Saul said to David, "You are not able to go against this Philistine to fight with him, for you are but a youth, and he has been a man of war from his youth." But David said to Saul, "Your servant used to keep sheep for his father. And when there came a lion, or a bear, and took a lamb from the flock, I went after him and struck him and delivered it out of his mouth. And if he arose against me, I caught him by his beard and struck him and killed him.

Your servant has struck down both lions and bears, and this uncircumcised Philistine shall be like one of them, for he has defied the armies of the living God." And David said, "The Lord who delivered me from the paw of the lion and from the paw of the bear will deliver me from the hand of this Philistine." (1 Sam. 17:32-37)

David is determined to confront Goliath and his armies. In fact, David did not wait for another invitation, he grabbed his sling and stones and he "approached the Philistine" (17:40). Unlike Saul, David confronts his people's enemy directly and says:

"You come to me with a sword and with a spear and with a javelin, but I come to you in the name of the Lord of hosts, the God of the armies of Israel, whom you have defied. This day the Lord will deliver you into my hand, and I will strike you down and cut off your head. And I will give the dead bodies of the host of the Philistines this day to the birds of the air and to the wild beasts of the earth, that all the earth may know that there is a God in Israel." (1 Sam. 17:45-47).

As we all know, David kills Goliath with a sling and a stone. But he doesn't end there. He runs to the fallen giant, removes his sword from its sheath, stabs Goliath and then decapitates him. What was the impact upon God's people? Their fear was removed and their aggression toward evil was righteously stimulated. The text says:

> "And the men of Israel and Judah rose with a shout and pursued the Philistines as far as Gath and the gates of Ekron, so that the wounded Philistines fell on the way from Shaaraim as far as Gath and Ekron. And the people of Israel came back from chasing the Philistines, and they plundered their camp. And David took the head of the Philistine and brought it to Jerusalem, but he put his armor in his tent." (1 Sam. 17:52-54)

Unlike Saul, David demonstrated the aggressive, confident, and wise posture required to influence an army to righteously fight against God's enemies and follow his path in victory.

But the central biblical lesson of this historical encounter was not about bravery or courage, it was a foreshadow of the coming Christ. David overcoming and beheading Goliath—the enemy of God's Old Testament people—was an image of the coming Messiah who would overcome and behead the serpent of sin—the enemy of God's New Testament people. In the same way that David uses his enemy's own weapon to decapitate him, Christ would use His enemy's own weapon (death) to decapitate Satan.

Sinclair Ferguson speaks to this reality when he says, "Imagine, for a moment, the reaction of Hell to the death of Christ. Jesus was bound with the bands of death. What celebration and joy! God was defeated! Vengeance was the Devil's. But they reckoned without the wisdom of God. For Christ could not be held down by the bands of death. In fact, through death He was paralyzing the one who had the power of death, and He was setting His people free (Heb. 2:14-15). What seemed to be defeat was actually victory. The resurrection morning was Hell's gloomiest day. Satan saw the wisdom of God and tasted defeat."[20]

In the same way that God's Old Testament people rose with a shout and pursued the enemies of Israel, God's New Testament people are to rise with a shout and pursue the enemies of the church. Now, according to Scripture, our enemies are not flesh and blood; but rather we battle against the rulers, against the authorities, against the cosmic powers over this present darkness, against the spiritual forces of evil in the heavenly places (Eph. 6:12).

That is, we are not called to physically slaughter evil men but to spiritually slaughter evil forces, demonic influences, and wicked authorities. We do not fight with physical swords but with the sword of the Spirit—the Word of God—the Gospel.

---

20   Sinclair Ferguson. *A Heart for God* (Edinburgh: Banner of Truth, 1987).

The Apostle Paul says, "For the weapons of our warfare are not of the flesh but have divine power to destroy strongholds. We destroy arguments and every lofty opinion raised against the knowledge of God, and take every thought captive to obey Christ..." (2 Cor. 10:4-6).

In short, we do not sit idle in the face of evil. Proverbs 8:13 says, "The fear of the LORD is hatred of evil." We do not stand behind a victorious Messiah and allow the enemies of God to mock His cause. We do not shut our mouths when it comes to the obedience of the Gospel. We are to proclaim the Good News of Christ's victory. We are to uphold the moral Law of God in our communities. What we don't do is allow the gates of Hell to hold back the church (Ps. 24:1).

Jesus says that upon Peter's confession that He is the Christ, He will build His church, and, "the gates of Hell shall not prevail against it" (Matt. 16:18). Too often, we forget that the church is not on the defensive, fighting a losing battle. We are on the *offensive*, always conquering through Christ. Like a mustard seed, the Kingdom of God will never shrink but will continue to expand until Christ subdues all that is His (Matt. 13:31-32; Mal. 1:11).

Jesus confirms that He has secured victory and has been given total and complete rule of the universe when He says, "All power is given to me, in heaven, and in earth. Go therefore, and teach all nations, baptizing them in the name of the

Father, and the Son, and the holy Ghost, teaching them to observe all things, whatsoever I have commanded you: and lo, I am with you alway, until the end of the world, amen" (Matt. 28:18-20, Geneva Version).

Jesus has won the war, but the battle rages on. He has not abandoned us but remains with us! We are to have no fear as one standing behind Saul but are to be fearless as one standing behind the Davidic King—the Messiah. He is the One reigning from heaven—commanding His people. He is the one growing His Kingdom through His Gospel. He is the one establishing dominion over His enemies. And Paul reminds us that He will not stop because "He must reign *until* He has put all His enemies under His feet" (1 Cor. 15:25).

In short, the battle in this world is not even close to being over. There is still much ground to take. There is still evil in this world that must be replaced with the righteousness of God. There are still pagan shrines that must be torn down. But most of all, there are still enemies of God—children of wrath—who must be converted to Christ's reign through the proclamation of the Gospel.

The takeaway lesson for the modern church is this: In war, an army follows the example of their King. Because of Christ, we are not cowards but conquerors! If we believe Jesus is merely the gentle and lowly Lamb but not the victorious and conquering Lion, we will be overrun in our tolerance of sin and ashamed in our inactivity toward evil.

Yes, we are to express the Gospel in love. Yes, we are to exude gentleness. Yes, we are to walk with humility and compassion toward others. But we are also to stand firm for truth and sharply against evil.

Furthermore, we must, by God's grace, advance the cause of Christ. We must saturate our cities with the Good News of Jesus and the moral Law of God. We must, as men, approach the world system by engaging society with biblical ethics. We must find God-honoring wives and raise God-glorifying children. We must start businesses and buy land and plant trees. We must infiltrate and ascertain political and civil influence. We must build ministries and print Bibles. We must establish schools, and plant churches.

The question then becomes, what are you doing? Are you watching King Jesus decapitate sin and remaining still? Are you hunkering down and waiting for Jesus to come and save you from this world? Or, are you joining the ranks of the living God's armies to claim the territory won by your Lord? Let us not overlook the fact that a triumphant King begets a triumphant people. Therefore, stand up and follow your Lord into the battlefield.

CHAPTER

08

The Call to Reform

THE CALL TO REFORM

I opened this book with a story of my father and how I noticed that courageous acts were often marked by succinct statements of responsibility.

I noted that the most courageous words ever spoken were by Jesus in Matthew 20:18 when He said, "Behold, we are going up to Jerusalem." It was these words that marked the transition from Christ's general ministry to His passion ministry (the cross). "We are going up to Jerusalem" really meant, "I am going to die for you, suffer the wrath of God for you, and be separated from my Father for you." Now, with context, we can grasp how intense these words truly were. He was marching toward the "hour" for which He had come (John 12:27). The Gospels repeatedly display His resolve. Jesus says, "The son of man must be lifted up." Mark 8:31 states, "And He began to teach them that the Son of Man must suffer many things…" In Luke 24:44, Jesus says, "My words which I spoke to you while

I was still with you, that all things which are written about Me in the Law of Moses and the Prophets and the Psalms must be fulfilled."

Jesus was on a mission. He was marching. He was leading. He was bold. He was fearless. He was sacrificial. He was resolved. He was, at this moment, carrying out the most masculine act in the history of the world.

Without reservation, we must be able to agree that the narrative of Christianity is not predominantly feminine. It includes women. It elevates women. It adores women. It honors women. It protects women. But from the patriarchs and the prophets to the Messiah and the Apostles, the accounts of Scripture are predominantly masculine. The Bible is filled with robust acts of faithful men. It has mission and war and courage. What it does not have is a collection of effeminate men. For this reason, we must examine why the church does. We must push against the feminization of our congregations. We must reject songs, programs, artwork, media, and preaching that disproportionately favors "gentle Jesus" while ignoring His masculinity, His judgments, and His rule and authority.

We must see the gap between the intense and costly Christianity seen in the Scriptures and frail and *costless* Christianity seen in our modern age. We must find a way to restore align-ment, to honor the masculinity of Christ and His men in the local church. We must reform the church's view of manhood. For when men and women fall into their proper place, the glory of God shines with radiance. In a world that can feel cold and dark, finding the kindling to spark this flame will permit the church and her Gospel to burn brightly before a confused world.

BIBLIOGRAPHY

Alexander, Lori (@godlywomanhood). 2022. "Twitter post." Twitter, April 15, 2022, 7:54 a.m. https://twitter.com/godlywomanhood/status/1514980570333425670?s=21&t=BPqLvpjJOaLe9i4TGIaqcg.

Aristotle. Nicomachean Ethics. Translated by H. Rackham. Loeb Classical Library 73. Cambridge, MA: Harvard University Press, 1926.

Bainton, Roland H., *Here I Stand: A Life of Martin Luther* (Nashville: Abington Press, 2013).

Bell, Debra, "Debate: Should Women Fight in War," U.S. News & World Report, February 13, 1978. Digital Version: https://www.usnews.com/news/blogs/press-past/2013/05/15/arguing-for-and-against-women-incombat-in-1978.

Boer, Paul A., *St. Ignatius of Antioch* (Create Space Publishing, 2012).

Brasher, Brenda E., *Godly Women: Fundamentalism and Female Power* (Chicago, IL: Rutgers University Press, 1997).

Brown, Curtis, "We Shall Fight on the Beaches," International Churchill Society, https://winstonchurchill.org/resources/speeches/1940-the-finest-hour/we-shall-fight-on-the-beaches/.

Calvin, John. 2022. Commentary, Vol. 1: On the Epistles of Paul the Apostle to the Corinthians (Classic Reprint). London, England: Forgotten Books.

Chesterton, G.K., "War and Politics," The Society of G.K. Chesterton, Originally said in the Illustrated London News, Jan. 14, 1911, https://www.chesterton.org/quotations/war-and-politics/.

Chrysostom, John. n.d. "Homily 24 on Romans." Newadvent.org. Accessed May 19, 2023. https://www.newadvent.org/fathers/210224.htm.

Edwards, Jonathan, *Religious Affections* (Moscow, ID: Canon Press, 2020).

Fahmy, Dalia, "Christian women in the U.S. are more religious than their male counterparts", Pew Research, April 6, 2018, https://www.pewresearch.org/fact-tank/2018/04/06/christian-women-in-the-u-s-are-more-religious-than-their-male-counterparts/.

Ferguson, Sinclair, *Grow in Grace* (Carlisle, PA: Banner of Truth, 1989), 33- 34.

Ferguson, Sinclair, *A Heart for God* (Edinburgh: Banner of Truth, 1987).

Handelsman, David J., Hirschberg, Angelica L., and Stephane, "Circulating Testosterone as the Hormonal Basis of Sex Differences in Athletic Performance" NCBI, July 13, 2018, https://www.ncbi.nlm.nih.gov/pmc/articles/PMC6391653/#__ffn_sectitle.

Miller, J.R., "The Manliness of Jesus" GraceGems.org, https://www.gracegems.org/Miller/manliness_of_jesus.htm. See also fwrobertson.org for a collection of his 19th century sermons.

Murrow, David, *Why Men Hate Going to Church* (Nashville: Thomas Nelson, 2011).

Roberts, Alastair, "Man and Woman in Creation (Genesis 1 and 2)", 9Marks, December 10, 2019, https://www.9marks.org/article/man-and-woman-in-creation-genesis-1-and-2/.

Stott, John, *The Cross of Christ* (Downers Grove, IL: Intervarsity Press, 2006), 37.
Trust, Gary "Ariana Grande Hits No. 1 On Pop Songs Chart With 'God Is a Woman,' Goes Top 10 With 'Breathin,' Billboard", https://www.billboard.com/pro/ariana-grande-god-is-a-woman-no-1-pop-songs-chart/.

Wedgeworth, Steven. 2018. Calvinist International. What is Effeminacy? July 2018. https://calvinistinternational.com/2018/07/15/what-is-effeminacy/.

Wikipedia, "Toxic Masculinity," 2020, https://en.m.wikipedia.org/wiki/Toxic_masculinity.

Shop.Relearn.org

OTHER TITLES BY DALE PARTRIDGE

———

HEADSHIP &
HEADCOVERING

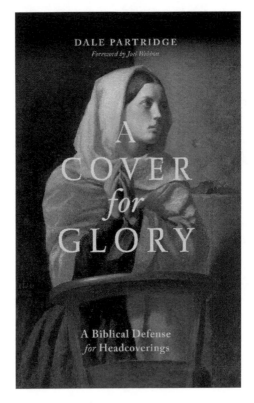

Relearn.org/Glory

AN INTRODUCTION TO
THEOLOGY

Relearn.org/Theology

AFFIRM YOUR CHILD'S GOD-GIVEN GENDER

Relearn.org/Gender

READ THE
GOSPEL

A Simple Presentation of

THE
GOSPEL

A MESSAGE
of LOVE

FINDING FORGIVENESS, FREEDOM, & FAMILY

MailtheGospel.org